I Spy Easter

BOOK FOR K|DS AGES 2-5

A Fun Guessing Game and Coloring Activity Book for Little Kids

Johnny B. Good

I Spy Easter Book for Kids Ages 2-5
Johnny B.Good © 2021
All Rights Reserved

I SPY
coloring book
for Kids
This book belongs to:

Thank you for getting our book!

If you find this coloring book fun and useful, we would be very grateful if you posted a short review! Your support does make a difference and we read every review personally.

If you would like to leave a review, just head on over to this book's Amazon page and click "Write a customer review".

Thank you for your support!

Johnny

I SPY WITH MY LITTLE EYE SOMETHING STARTING WITH...

A = April

I SPY WITH MY LITTLE EYE SOMETHING STARTING WITH...

B= Basket

I SPY WITH MY LITTLE EYE SOMETHING STARTING WITH...

C = Chick

I SPY WITH MY LITTLE EYE SOMETHING STARTING WITH...

D= Duckling

I SPY WITH MY LITTLE EYE SOMETHING STARTING WITH...

E= Eggs

I SPY WITH MY LITTLE EYE SOMETHING STARTING WITH...

F = Family

I SPY WITH MY LITTLE EYE SOMETHING STARTING WITH...

G = Grass

I SPY WITH MY LITTLE EYE SOMETHING STARTING WITH...

H = Holy

I SPY WITH MY LITTLE EYE SOMETHING STARTING WITH...

I = Ice cream

I SPY WITH MY LITTLE EYE SOMETHING STARTING WITH...

J= Jellybeans

I SPY WITH MY LITTLE EYE SOMETHING STARTING WITH...

K = King

I SPY WITH MY LITTLE EYE SOMETHING STARTING WITH...

L= Lamb

I SPY WITH MY LITTLE EYE SOMETHING STARTING WITH...

M=
Marshmallow

I SPY WITH MY LITTLE EYE SOMETHING STARTING WITH...

N= Nest

I SPY WITH MY LITTLE EYE SOMETHING STARTING WITH...

O= Olive branch

I SPY WITH MY LITTLE EYE SOMETHING STARTING WITH...

P= Plastic Eggs

I SPY WITH MY LITTLE EYE SOMETHING STARTING WITH...

Q= Queen

I SPY WITH MY LITTLE EYE SOMETHING STARTING WITH...

R= Rabbit

I SPY WITH MY LITTLE EYE SOMETHING STARTING WITH...

S= Spring

I SPY WITH MY LITTLE EYE SOMETHING STARTING WITH...

T= Turkey

I SPY WITH MY LITTLE EYE SOMETHING STARTING WITH...

U = Unicorn

I SPY WITH MY LITTLE EYE SOMETHING STARTING WITH...

V= Vacation

I SPY WITH MY LITTLE EYE SOMETHING STARTING WITH...

W= Watermelon

I SPY WITH MY LITTLE EYE SOMETHING STARTING WITH...

X= Xylophone

I SPY WITH MY LITTLE EYE SOMETHING STARTING WITH...

I SPY WITH MY LITTLE EYE SOMETHING STARTING WITH...

Z = Zoo

Happy Easter

I hope you enjoyed this book!

This is a fun and simple way to make reading a process that is fun, natural, and interesting!

It is also a way of creating special moments with children, a precious keepsake at any age.

If you think that this book has been helpful, <u>please leave a review</u> and help other customers make the right choice...

Thank You!

Also by Johnny B. Good

COLOR BY NUMBER BOOK FOR GIRLS
Unicorn, Mermaids and Other Cute Animals Coloring Book for Kids Ages 4-8

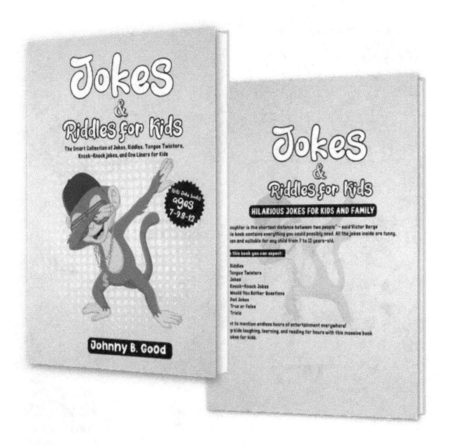

JOKES & RIDDLES FOR KIDS
The Smart Collection Of Jokes, Riddles, Tongue Twisters, and funniest Knock-Knock Jokes Ever

WOULD YOU RATHER
A Hilarious and Interactive Question Game Book For Kids

CPSIA information can be obtained
at www.ICGtesting.com
Printed in the USA
BVHW012150110322
631324BV00013B/463